LEWIS AND CLARK

BY BONNIE SACHATELLO-SAWYER

SCHOLASTIC

PROFESSIONAL BOOKS

New York • Toronto • London • Auckland • Sydney

DEDICATION
For my beloved grandparents,
Joseph and Rose Sachatello and Winton and Dorothy Rowan

ACKNOWLEDGMENTS
This book would not have been possible without the expertise and assistance of many, including Duncan Bullock, Virginia Dooley, Ken Karsmizki, Barbara Kubik, Ann Lockie, Larry Mensching, Beth Merrick, Dr. Gary Moulton, Don Nell, Suzanne Sachatello, Gordon and Betty Strachan, Bruce Selyem, Jean Thorson, Jane Warner, and Robert Yaw.

A special thanks to the Lewis and Clark Trail Heritage Foundation, Inc.

Scholastic Inc. grants teachers permission to photocopy the activity pages from this book for classroom use. No other part of this publication may be reproduced in whole or in part, or stored in a retrieval system, or transmitted in any form or by any means, electronic, mechanical, photocopying, recording, or otherwise, without written permission of the publisher. For information regarding permission, write to Scholastic Inc., 555 Broadway, New York, NY 10012.

Excerpts from *The Journals of Lewis and Clark*, edited by Bernard DeVoto, Houghton Mifflin Company, 1953. By permission of Houghton Mifflin Company.

Excerpts from *The Journals of Lewis and Clark Expedition* Volumes 2, 4, and 5, edited by Gary E. Moulton, University of Nebraska Press, 1993. By permission of University of Nebraska Press.

Site Stratigraphy activity adapted from *Intrigue of the Past: A Teacher's Activity Guide for Fourth through Seventh Grades*. This publication is a joint project of the Utah Interagency Task Force on Cultural Resources.

Cover Art: *Lewis and Clark at Celilo Falls*

Photo Credits: Lewis and Clark Trail Heritage Foundation: Pages 22, 23, 33, 44, 48, 56; National Geographic Society: Pages 3, 8, 10, 21; Museum of the Rockies, Montana State University: Pages 12, 24, 38, 46, 56, 57, 59; Joslyn Art Museum: Pages 55, 58; U.S. Department of Interior: Page 45; Independence National Historical Park: Page 7; Jefferson National Expansion Memorial, St. Louis, Mo.: Pages 32, 35; Montana Historical Society: Page 36.

Cover design by Jaime Lucero and Vincent Ceci
Interior design by Vincent Ceci and Drew Hires
Interior illustrations by Drew Hires

TABLE OF CONTENTS

INTRODUCTION

A Note from the LEWIS AND CLARK TRAIL HERITAGE FOUNDATION

Dear Readers:

The story of the bold journey of the Lewis and Clark expedition in 1803-06 remains a classic in the annals of exploration histories. It is an epic adventure that reflects the democratic ideals, the enthusiasm, and the energy of a new nation in a new century.

The journey began when President Thomas Jefferson directed Captain Meriwether Lewis and Captain William Clark to undertake a mission of exploration through the newly acquired Louisiana Territory and the Pacific Northwest. The two men recruited privates, officers, volunteers, guides, and interpreters and molded them into a "Corps of Discovery."

Six members of the corps recorded the details of their journey. They described their rigorous training, the strict military discipline, the challenges of the climate and the terrain, the hunger, and the fatigue. They spoke of encounters with Native Americans, the beauty of nature, as well as the moments of laughter, sorrow, enthusiasm, and awe they shared. "We proceeded on," they often wrote—and proceed they did. For more than two years they trekked—up the Missouri River, across the Rocky Mountains, down the Snake and Columbia rivers to the Pacific Ocean, and eventually back to St. Louis.

To study the Lewis and Clark expedition today is to study the landscape, the people, and the events of an epic journey that, although it took place hundreds of years ago, serves as a reminder that what was important to these explorers then is still important to us today—teamwork, consensus, appreciation of diversity, sharing, and hard work.

May your journey through the story of the expedition be as wondrous and as rewarding as it was for Lewis, Clark, and their fellow explorers.

Clyde G. Sid Huggins

Clyde G. "Sid" Huggins
President, 1996-97
Lewis and Clark Trail Heritage Foundation, Inc.

For additional information write to:

> The Lewis and Clark Trail Heritage Foundation, Inc.
> PO Box 3434
> Great Falls, MT 59404

HOW TO USE THIS BOOK

We hope the activities and projects in this book will inspire students to learn more about this very significant event in United States history. Here are a few tips to consider before getting started.

Invite students to help design your Lewis and Clark theme unit.

A KWL (Know / Want to Know / Learned) chart will assist you in determining what students really want to know about the expedition (see page 9). For example, they may want to know more about individual crew members and what they did before and after the journey. Give students an opportunity to contribute their ideas and see what happens.

Use this resource—in combination with the journals—to motivate your students, and focus your theme unit accordingly.

The Journals of Lewis and Clark, edited by Bernard DeVoto, is available through most bookstores and found in many libraries. Have students read aloud and discuss portions of the actual journals every day during this theme unit. Because this book is set up to parallel the expedition, you can use corresponding journal entries as a starting place for any of the activities.

Encourage students to read more about the expedition.

Try setting up a classroom library of nonfiction titles, appropriate for many reading levels. (See the Resource List on the inside back cover for some suggestions.) Parents, the school librarian, and local history buffs may be able to help you. Give students time to read these books—and the journals—along the way.

Encourage students to demonstrate what they have learned by assigning a culminating activity.

Invite students to conclude their studies of Lewis and Clark by coming up with an original research project of their own. For example, they may want to learn more about one of the expedition members, or create a model of one of the forts or boats the crew built based on the information provided in the journals.

Follow the route of Lewis and Clark where possible.

Today the trail can be explored by boat, car, or foot. You can also learn about the expedition from the many museum exhibits and interpretive signs found along the way. See a list of resources on the inside back cover. Additional information can be obtained by writing the Lewis and Clark Trail Heritage Foundation. Their address is on the inside back cover.

Part 1

Why Go West?

MERIWETHER LEWIS

WILLIAM CLARK

BACKGROUND INFORMATION

What Was the Louisiana Territory?

The Louisiana Territory was a large piece of land that stretched from the Mississippi River to the west side of the Rocky Mountains. When the United States purchased it from France in 1803, the size of the United States increased by 140 percent, or more than doubled in size. This territory was later subdivided into the states of Missouri, Nebraska, Iowa, Arkansas, North and South Dakota, Louisiana, Kansas, Minnesota, Montana, Wyoming, Colorado, and Oklahoma.

Why Did the United States Purchase the Louisiana Territory?

Long before President Thomas Jefferson was able to secure the purchase of the Louisiana Territory, he recognized its value. Indians were known to collect handsome furs and pelts and transport them through this region even during the winter months. The lure of furs led Jefferson to believe that, if the United States owned the Louisiana Territory, America would dominate the fur-trade business. He also hoped that the territory would contain a river route that would enable goods to be moved up the Mississippi all the way to the Pacific Ocean. At the time, supplies had to be shipped completely around the southern tip of South America. Jefferson was determined to learn all he could about the new territory—from its landforms to its inhabitants to its potential for trade.

The purchase of the Louisiana Territory was to become one of the most important transactions in United States history. Not only did it provide a great deal of land filled with rich mineral and animal resources, but the acquisition protected America from invasion from the west.

It also made the later acquisition of Oregon and the Spanish Territory (later to become the states of California, Arizona, New Mexico, and Texas) inevitable.

Who Were Lewis and Clark?

Meriwether Lewis was a young military man at the time he was appointed to be President Jefferson's private secretary in 1800. In this position, Lewis was often invited to Jefferson's home at Monticello to learn more about astronomy, botany, cartography, geology, Indian affairs, mineralogy, and navigation. It was clear that he was in training to lead a major expedition of the West. On June 20, 1803, President Thomas Jefferson wrote an official letter to Lewis detailing what he wanted him to accomplish as head of a scientific expedition into the Louisiana Territory. The expedition was to seek out a river route to the Pacific Ocean and collect as much information as it could about this vast new land.

Expedition Fun Facts!

◆ For the Louisiana Territory, the United States government paid France $15 million, which is roughly three cents an acre.

◆ President Jefferson thought that giant woolly mammoths might live in the foothills of the Rocky Mountains.

◆ Congress approved $2,500 for the expedition. The final cost totaled over $40,000.

◆ Lewis had a dried soup made that was packed in canisters. After the explorers ate the soup, they melted down the canisters to make bullets.

The President wanted detailed maps as well as accurate notes about everything the explorers saw—plants, minerals, wildlife, and different Native American groups. To accomplish this, Jefferson sent Lewis to Philadelphia for more training in biology, astronomy, and medicine.

Lewis then asked his close friend William Clark to help with the expedition. Clark had once been his commanding officer in the army. Where Lewis had a great deal of scientific expertise, Clark had experience communicating with various Native American groups and organizing large numbers of men. Clark was considered to be more outgoing while Lewis was more thoughtful and reflective.

How Did Lewis and Clark Prepare for the Expedition?

Lewis gathered most of the supplies for the trip. He went to the United States government arsenal in Harper's Ferry, West Virginia, to acquire knives, tomahawks, rifles, flints, and gunpowder packed in waterproof lead containers. These lead containers would later be melted down to make lead balls.

Lewis and Clark also gathered together the men who would travel with them in 1803. They are listed on the poster. They included fourteen soldiers, nine volunteers, an interpreter, and Clark's slave, York. An additional seven soldiers and nine river men were to join the group for the first part of the trip. Together, this expedition team was called the Corps of Discovery.

In Lancaster, Pennsylvania, Lewis bought scientific equipment and studied celestial observation with an astronomer. He traveled on to Philadelphia to purchase more guns and clothing and dozens of gifts for the people they would encounter along the way. These gifts included tomahawks, knives, scissors, mirrors, brooches, calico shirts, and rings. He also received medical advice and supplies from Benjamin Rush, a well-respected doctor.

Between December 1803 and May 1804, Clark trained the Corps of Discovery while Lewis continued to gather trip supplies. On a rainy May morning in 1804, the corps finally started their expedition up the Missouri River.

What Was Happening In 1803?

◆ The United States celebrated its 20th birthday.

◆ The second United States census recorded 5,300,000 Americans including almost 900,000 slaves.

◆ Scientist Joseph Priestly identified oxygen.

◆ The first tax-supported public library opened.

◆ Shoes began to be designed specifically for right and left feet.

◆ Johnny Appleseed was hard at work giving away and selling apple trees.

LEWIS AND CLARK KWL CHART

This learning tool serves as the perfect springboard to a unit on the Lewis and Clark expedition. It gives you the opportunity to both determine students' prior knowledge and choose learning activities based on topics that they want to know more about. A KWL chart (**K**: Kids tell what they **know**; **W**: Kids tell what they **want** to know; **L**: Kids tell what they've **learned**) will help to ensure that your study of the Lewis and Clark expedition is learner-centered—and exciting!

MATERIALS
✔ reproducible on page 14
✔ masking tape

DIRECTIONS

1. Use masking tape to divide a large wall space into three columns, making the third column about twice as large as each of the other two (see below). Label the first "What we know about the Lewis and Clark expedition"; the second, "What we want to know about the expedition"; and the third, "What we have learned about the expedition."

K	W	L

2. Invite students to brainstorm facts they already know about the Lewis and Clark expedition, such as "They explored the western United States" or "Sacagawea went with them." Record each fact on Lewis' silhouette. (See page 14 for a reproducible pattern.) Tape it in the first column.

3. Invite students to brainstorm questions they would like to have answered, such as "What did Lewis and Clark discover?" or "Did anyone leave the expedition?" Record each question on Lewis's silhouette and tape it in the second column.

4. Now it's time to get cracking at the answers to those intriguing questions. Over the course of the unit, each time the class arrives at an answer, have students write the new fact on Lewis's silhouette and hang it in the "What we have learned" column. (The facts you add to the third column need not be limited to the questions asked.)

At the close of your unit, revisit the KWL chart by having students help you read each fact relating to Lewis and Clark. You'll be amazed at what the class has learned!

CHECKING YOUR FACTS

All too often, books and movies reinforce historical myth rather than fact. To help students distinguish fact from fantasy and to check their prior knowledge of American history, start your unit off with a quiz on Lewis and Clark. (See page 15 for a reproducible quiz.) This quiz is designed to help spark your students' interest while they recall prior knowledge.

EXPEDITION GOALS

On June 20, 1803, President Thomas Jefferson wrote a letter to Captain Meriwether Lewis detailing the goals of the expedition. (See page 11.) Read this letter aloud. Ask a student to make a list of the tasks that Jefferson asked Lewis to accomplish. Discuss as a class Jefferson's reasons for sending an expedition to explore Louisiana. Make a list of any new vocabulary words.

BUYING SUPPLIES

One of the most difficult choices that Lewis and Clark had to make was what to bring along with them. Supplies were chosen based on their importance to the expedition's overall mission. An item's size, weight, durability, and value to the team's health and well-being also had to be taken into account. Provide students with a copy of the reproducible found on page 16 and let them match their pre-expedition shopping skills with those of Lewis and Clark. (Answers are on page 63.)

WOULD YOU GO?

Traveling into unknown territory posed a tremendous challenge to Lewis and Clark. It was certainly not a trip for the timid. Challenge students to think about the level of risk they would be willing to take by responding to Lewis's invitation to join the expedition. (See the reproducible on page 17.)

MAKING SENSE OF MAPS

In 1803, parts of what would eventually become the United States were occupied by England, France, Russia, and Spain. Political boundaries were established by countries as land was bought, sold, seized through wars, or traded. To help students understand the political boundaries of our country prior to Lewis and Clark's expedition, try the mapping projects that begin on page 12.

Partial Letter from Thomas Jefferson to Meriwether Lewis:

The object of your mission is to explore the Missouri River, & such principal stream of it, as, by it's course and communication with the waters of the Pacific Ocean, whether the Columbia, Oregan, Colorado or any other river may offer the most direct & practicable water-communication across the continent for the purpose of commerce.

Beginning at the mouth of the Missouri, you will take observations of latitude & longitude, at all remarkable points on the river, & especially at the mouths of rivers, at rapids, at islands, & other places & objects distinguished by such natural marks & characters of a durable kind, as that they may with certainty be recognised hereafter....Your observations are to be taken with great pains & accuracy....Several copies of these as well as of your notes should be made at leisure times, & put into the care of the most trust-worthy of your attendants, to guard, by multiplying them, against the accidental losses to which they will be exposed.

You will therefore endeavor to make yourself acquainted...with the names of the nations and their numbers; the extent & limits of their possessions, their relations with other tribes of nations; their language, traditions, monuments....

Other objects worthy of notice will be the soil & face of the country, its growth & vegetable productions, especially those not of the U.S., the animals of the country generally, & especially...the remains or accounts of any which may be deemed rare or extinct; the mineral productions of every kind; volcanic appearances; climate, times of appearance of particular birds, reptiles or insects.

To provide, on the accident of your death, against anarchy, dispersion, & the consequent danger to your party, and total failure of the enterprize, you are hereby authorised...to name the person among them who shall succeed to the command on your decease....

Given under my hand at the City of Washington, this 20th day of June, 1803.

Thomas Jefferson
President of the United States

MATERIALS

✔ reproducible on page 18

DIRECTIONS

1. As an introductory activity, invite students to draw from memory a map of the United States. Have them trace the boundaries of as many states as possible, put the Missouri and Mississippi rivers in their correct places, draw in the Appalachian and Rocky mountains, and label several major cities. Give students a chance to share their maps with the class.

2. Invite students to identify the states and territories that existed in 1803 by using the reproducible found on page 18. Have them choose a color for each territory and then use the same color for the map. To extend this activity, encourage students to research the difference between a state and a territory. When were each of the states established?

MAKE A RELIEF MAP

Lewis and Clark knew very little about the land west of the Mississippi River. For example, they believed that the Rocky Mountains were much smaller than they actually are.

The physical geography of the United States is determined by the geologic forces that shaped it. To create a giant relief map of the United States, start by reproducing the relief map found on page 19. Using an overhead projector, enlarge the map until it is three feet wide. Then trace the map onto a large piece of cardboard or tag board. Using the dough recipe that follows, make enough dough so that your class can sculpt the physical features of the country.

MATERIALS

✔ reproducible on page 19
✔ cardboard, tag board, or heavy cardboard
✔ a small box of toothpicks
✔ spoon
    Dough recipe
✔ 6 cups of salt
✔ 6 cups of flour
✔ 3 cups of water

Mix together the salt and flour. Then add the water slowly and stir until the dough is well mixed.

DIRECTIONS

1. Give a group of students 3 cups of the dough mixture. Have them start by outlining and building up the mountain ranges marked on the map. Then have them fill in the rest of the map using the remaining dough. The rivers can be marked by making an indentation with toothpicks, spoons, or craft sticks.

2. Set the map in a warm place to dry. (This may take as long as a week.) Then invite students to paint the landforms using acrylic paints. This map can be used throughout your theme unit. See activities on pages 23 and 47.

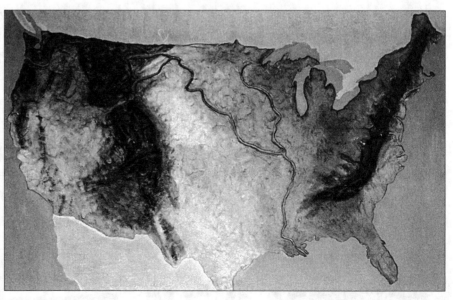

■ *To Extend Learning*

Reproduce a copy of a local city map that shows your school. Have each student write directions from the school grounds to another place on the map. Invite students to give their directions to a friend. Using the map, see how many students can follow one another's written instructions. Follow up with a discussion about the importance of accurately recording information. How important were accurate maps and guides to the Lewis and Clark expedition? Good maps of the region did not exist at the time. Clark made very accurate maps along the way, and when he returned he asked later travelers for more information.

MAKE AND USE A SEXTANT

Lewis taught himself to use survey instruments prior to the expedition. Instruments available at the time included measuring chains (for determining distance), a chronometer (a ship's clock that enabled Lewis to calculate longitude), a sextant (to measure angles), a level, a quadrant, and a compass. Students can measure the altitude of objects, similar to the way Lewis did, by making a simple sextant.

A sextant measures the angle between whatever you are looking at relative to the place you are taking the measurement. It can be used to determine the heights of objects in the distance, e.g., mountains, hills, or knolls. This information can then be used to generate topographical maps.

MATERIALS
✔ reproducible on page 20
✔ cardboard
✔ scissors
✔ 24-inch-long piece of string (one for each student)
✔ small pieces of chalk or erasers (to be used as small weights)

DIRECTIONS

1. Have each student cut out the sextant pattern and glue it to a piece of cardboard. Once the glue is dry, trim the cardboard to the edges of the sextant pattern.

2. Help each student tie a knot close to one end of the piece of string. Then have them thread the string through the hole so that the knot is on the reverse side of the pattern. Finally, have them tie the weight (an eraser works well) on the other end of the thread.

3. To use the sextant, invite students to sight in an object by looking along the top edge. Next, have students carefully move the sextant away from their face and read the angle where the string touches the sextant. This is the altitude of the object relative to the ground.

4. To help students get started measuring the altitude of objects, have them stand at several points in the room and sight in the classroom door. Invite them to share their results. Does it matter where they are standing in the room? Why? Next, invite students to measure the angle of the top of a bulletin board. If possible, go outdoors and measure the angle of trees or other prominent landmarks.

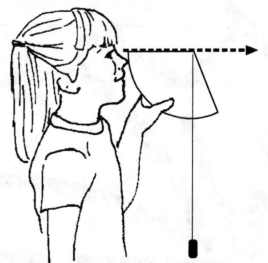

LEWIS SILHOUETTE

Reproduce this silhouette to use with the KWL chart.

CHECKING YOUR FACTS

Take the Lewis and Clark challenge! See how much you already know by answering the questions below. *Fill in the blanks.*

1. President _____ ordered Captain Meriwether Lewis to survey the Louisiana Territory.

2. The United States government purchased the Louisiana Territory from _____.

3. The Louisiana Territory stretched from the Mississippi River to the _____.

4. The United States paid _____ in order to acquire the Louisiana Territory.

5. At first the expedition moved slowly west along the _____ River.

Answer True or False.

6. _____ No person had ever seen the Louisiana Territory before the Lewis and Clark expedition.

7. _____ The United States government knew the exact size of the territory before it was purchased.

8. _____ Lewis and Clark were the first white men to venture into the Louisiana Territory.

9. _____ Lewis and Clark traveled by themselves as they explored Louisiana.

10. _____ The explorers brought gifts for any Native American groups they might meet along the way.

11. _____ The expedition lasted over two years.

12. _____ The purchase of the Louisiana Territory more than doubled the size of the United States.

13. _____ The expedition communicated with Native Americans by using a translator and sign language.

14. _____ This journey discouraged others from exploring America's western lands.

15. _____ The United States government paid for the Lewis and Clark expedition.

Name _____

BUYING SUPPLIES

The year is 1803. You've been asked to join Lewis and Clark's Corps of Discovery. You will be heading into unknown lands and can only take a limited amount of supplies. Most of the time, your supplies will be stored in a boat, but other times, you will have to carry them in a rucksack or pack them on a horse. On this page are a list of 18 items you might choose to take with you in 1803. You can only take 12. Which ones will you take? After you decide, your teacher will tell you what Lewis and Clark actually took.

SUPPLIES	Check the 12 items that you would take.
50 pounds of pork	
15 wooden chairs	
Art supplies	
Fishing line	
Firewood	
5 compasses	
2 medicine chests	
45 hand axes	
Insect repellent	
Oil cloth tents	
Spare clothing	
200 postage stamps	
Trumpets	
Gunpowder	
Ribbons and beads	
Blank paper	
5 cameras	
30 sheep skins	

WOULD YOU GO?

In 1803, Captain Meriwether Lewis wrote William Clark and asked him to join the expedition. William Clark knew that he would have to endure many hardships, but also that he would have a chance to see new places and discover new people, plants, and animals.

If you had been asked by Captain Lewis to travel with him to unknown lands, what would have been your response? Write your answer to Lewis below. Will you join him? Why or why not?

October 1803

Dear Captain Lewis,

_____

_____

_____

_____

_____

_____

_____

_____

_____

_____

_____

Sincerely,

_____

Unscramble the following letters to read Clark's response to Lewis.

"YM EDIRFN, I NOJI OUY TIWH DNAH NDA EHRAT"

_____

Name _____

MAKING SENSE OF MAPS

On this 1803 map, locate and identify the territories and states listed in the boxes below.
Then use markers or crayons to complete the map key.

Territory

Spanish Territory ☐

Oregon Territory ☐

Louisiana Purchase ☐

Indiana Territory ☐

Mississippi Territory ☐

State

Maine (ME)
Vermont (VT)
New Hampshire (NH)
Massachusetts (MA)
Connecticut (CT)
Rhode Island (RI)
New York (NY)
Maryland (MD)
Delaware (DE)
New Jersey (NJ)

Pennsylvania (PA)
Virginia (VA)
Ohio (OH)
Kentucky (KY)
Tennessee (TN)
Georgia (GA)
North Carolina (NC)
South Carolina (SC)
Florida (FL)

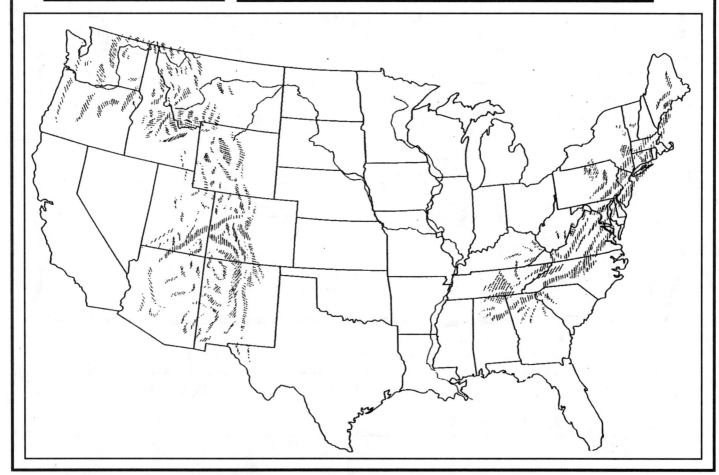

RELIEF MAP

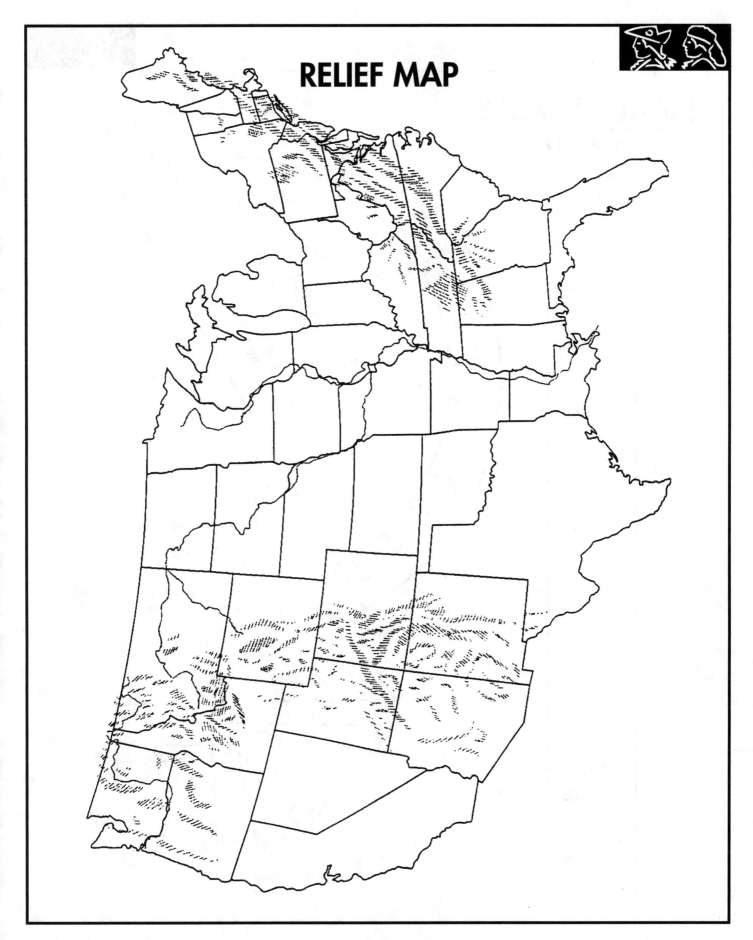

Name _____

MAKE AND USE A SEXTANT

Follow the directions your teacher gives you to make and use this sextant.

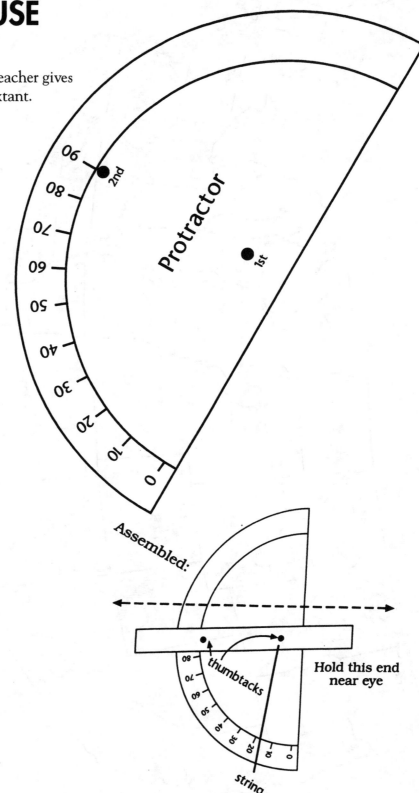

Part 2

Starting Out

What Route Did Lewis and Clark Choose?

In searching for a river route that would lead to the Pacific Ocean, Lewis and Clark decided to follow the Missouri River upstream. Based on the information they had from earlier travelers, they thought the mighty Missouri would lead them to the Northwest Passage. Early explorers believed that the Northwest Passage was a waterway through North America that linked the Atlantic and Pacific oceans. What Lewis and Clark found instead was a direct route over the Rocky Mountains that eventually led them to the Columbia River and the Pacific Ocean. They did not find the fabled Northwest Passage.

When Did the Expedition Start?

After gathering supplies, Lewis and Clark established a winter camp in 1803-04 at Camp Wood, just north of St. Louis along the Missouri River. At Camp Wood, they trained their men and made their final preparations.

On May 14, 1804, the expedition started up the Missouri River. The crew of 45 traveled in a long wooden keelboat and two small shallow boats called *pirogues*. As they were maneuvering upstream, the expedition members had to row or pole the boats upriver. Both the keelboat and pirogues had sails that could be used to move the boats upstream when the wind was blowing in the right direction. But such weather conditions were rare. Usually, the men poled or rowed, and where the current was especially strong, they dragged the boats upriver with ropes while walking on the riverbank. It was hard going. On a good day they traveled 15 miles.

How Did Lewis and Clark Document Their Experiences?

President Jefferson asked Lewis and Clark to carefully describe their experiences and record whatever they found. They did so by writing notes and drawing pictures in journals made of paper and leather. In Lewis's journal, he described the interesting animals and plants they encountered. Clark made detailed maps that later proved to be very accurate. After the expedition, their journal entries became the main source of information on western geography and wildlife for generations of future explorers.

STUDENT ACTIVITIES

READING FROM THE JOURNALS

To help students understand the expedition, have them read portions of Lewis and Clark's journals out loud every day. A good resource to use for this activity is *The Journals of Lewis and Clark*, edited by Bernard DeVoto. Select journal

entries from this book, and after your students have read through them, ask questions to stimulate discussion.

Sample questions for discussion:

◆ *According to their writings, what do Lewis and Clark suggest is important to them?*

◆ *How do the two explorers make decisions?*

◆ *How do they discipline others in the corps?*

◆ *Did they make any mistakes?*

◆ *What does it take to be a leader?*

◆ *What was a hardship?*

◆ *What was a favorite site?*

◆ *What different kinds of reactions did Lewis and Clark get from the Native Americans they encountered?*

◆ *What expectations did Lewis and Clark have?*

◆ *What was the most important thing they accomplished?*

PERSONAL JOURNALS

Have students begin writing a personal journal in the style of Lewis and Clark. During your unit, ask them periodically to record daily experiences, interactions with friends, impressions of school activities, and family matters. They may also want to tell what they are learning in their Lewis and Clark unit. To get started, help students assemble their own personal journals.

MATERIALS

✔ reproducibles on pages 25 and 26
✔ crayons or markers
✔ pencils
✔ staples and stapler

DIRECTIONS

1. Make enough copies of the journal cover and page so that each student has a front cover and four inside pages. Distribute the copies to

students and help them put their books together. With the cover on the outside, fold the pages in half and staple the seam.

2. Help motivate students to make daily journal entries by setting up a writing corner in your classroom. Put out some markers and crayons along with pencils. Prop up a sign with questions to help stimulate students to document their lives through writing and drawing.

3. Set aside at least ten minutes each day for students to write or draw in their journals. To encourage writing, establish a minimum number of words or sentences that need to be completed each day. When finished, have students leave their journals with you until the next day.

SPELLING TEST

Clark was not a particularly good speller. Using the activity on page 27, have students identify the misspelled words in the journal entry and provide the correct spelling.

MARKING YOUR MAPS

As you discuss significant historical events with your students, or they read about a noteworthy occurrence in *The Journals*, place a flag on your relief map as a reminder of the event's location.

MATERIALS
✔ reproducible on page 28
✔ toothpicks
✔ glue
✔ scissors

DIRECTIONS
1. Ask one student to cut out the flags and glue them onto the toothpicks. Note that key places are already listed on some of the flags and that one flag is blank so that you can add it where you see fit.

2. As you and your students discuss an event or place, mark the occasion by sticking the flag in your relief map.

DETAILED DESCRIPTIONS

When Lewis and Clark explored the West, photography had not yet been invented. To share unknown plants and animals, Lewis needed to describe new species in a way that others could understand. Whenever he could, he also made

detailed scientific illustrations. In this activity, challenge your students to do the same, and improve their writing and illustration skills in the process.

MATERIALS
✔ reproducible on page 29
✔ pencils

DIRECTIONS
Pass out the reproducible and encourage students to describe each of the pictures using as many adjectives as they can. When they are fin-

ished, have them share their descriptions with the class. Read aloud Lewis's descriptions, found on pages 63 and 64.

SCIENTIFIC ILLUSTRATION

Because Lewis and Clark trekked West without cameras or an artist, they needed to draw precise pictures of every new kind of plant and animal that they saw. Remember that Jefferson had instructed the explorers to take careful notes about every "object worthy of notice." To introduce your class to the art of scientific illustration, start by taking them outdoors.

Once outside, give each student two sheets of unlined paper and a pencil. Invite them to pick an object—such as a leaf, plant, or insect—and describe it on one sheet of paper. On the other sheet of paper, have students draw the object in detail.

When students are finished, gather together their illustrations and hang them around your classroom. Collect the descriptions and randomly pass them out to the class. Encourage students to match each description to an illustration.

READER'S THEATER

Help students appreciate the extraordinary travels of Lewis and Clark by encouraging them to research and write a play about the expedition based on *The Journals*. To get students started, reproduce and distribute the play found on pages 30 and 31, which they can continue. When it comes time for class performances, consider videotaping each play. A classroom "screening party" can be a fun culminating activity!

MORE MAPMAKING

It was Clark's responsibility to map the landscape. To further develop your students' understanding of cartography, set up this easy and fun mapmaking contest.

MATERIALS
✔ unlined white paper
✔ clipboards (or something to write on)
✔ pencils
✔ small objects (toys, pennies, erasers, etc.)

DIRECTIONS
1. To get started, discuss mapmaking with your students. What kind of information is important to know when making a map? What references do most mapmakers use to help orient others?

2. Following your discussion, take students to a park, if possible, or the school lawn. Pair off students into teams and have each one hide a small object and then draw a map to help locate it. Finally, ask the teams to switch maps and see if they can make their way to the hidden prize.

■ *To Extend Learning*
Collect a number of different kinds of maps. Pass them out and have students make a list of everything they have in common (e.g., titles, legends, scale of miles, directional stars, compass roses, and so on).

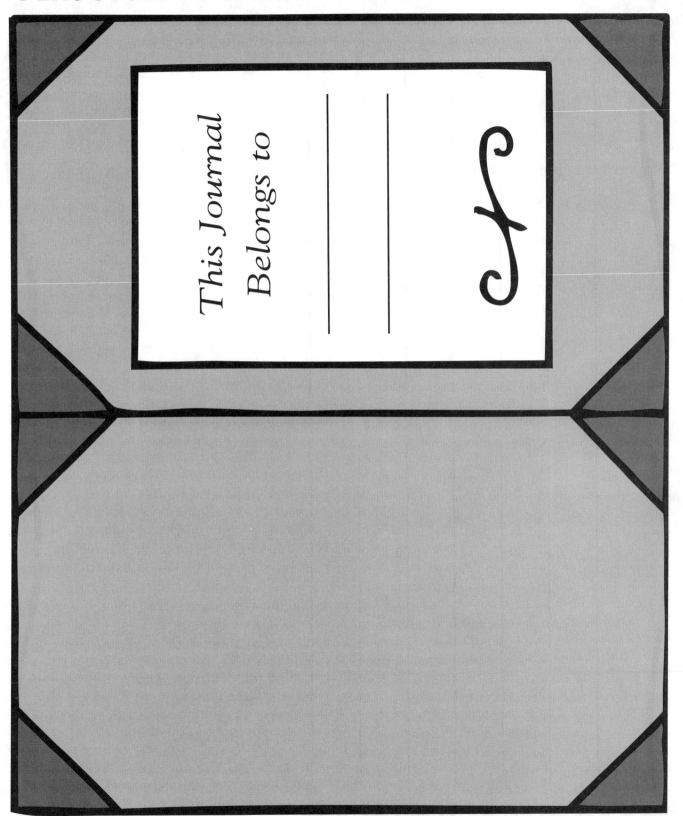

This Journal Belongs to

PERSONAL JOURNAL PAGES

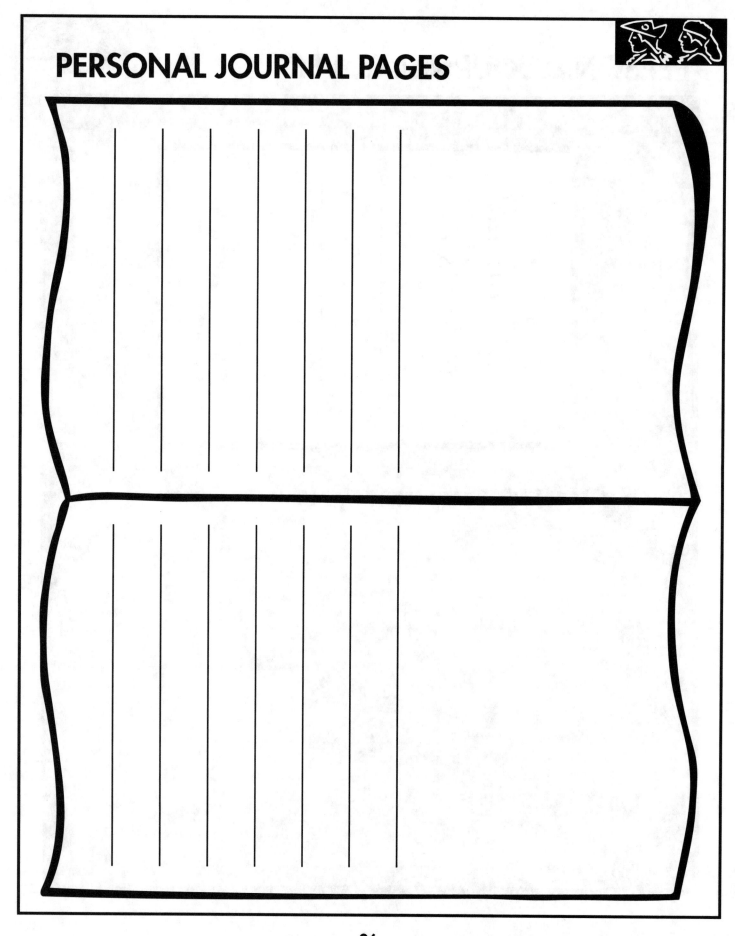

Name _____

SPELLING TEST

Circle the misspelled words in this journal entry by William Clark from *The Journals of Lewis and Clark*, edited by Bernard DeVoto. Below the journal entry, write the correct spelling in the space provided.

(Clark) August 20, 1805

Set out at half past 6 oClock and proceeded on (met maney parties of Indians)
thro' a hilley Countrey to the Camp of the Indians on a branch of the Columbia River, before
we entered this Camp a Serimonious hault was requested by the Chief and I smoked with all
that Came around, for Several pipes, we then proceeded on to the Camp & I was introduced
into the only Lodge they had which was pitched in the Center for my party all the other Lodges
made of bushes, after a fiew Indian Seremonies I informed the Indians the object of our journey
our good intentions towards them my Consirn for their distressed Situation, what we had done
for them in makeing a piece with the Minitarras Mandans Rickara &c. for them.and requested
them all to take over their horses & assist Capt. Lewis across &c. also informing them the
object of my journey down the river, and requested a guide to accompany me, all of which was
repeited by the Chief to the whole village.

Those poor people Could only raise a Sammon & a little dried Choke Cherries for us half the
men of the tribe with the Chief turned out to hunt the antilopes, at 3 oClock after giveing a fiew
Small articles as presents I set out accompanied by an old man as a Guide I endevered to
procure as much information from thos people as possible without much Suckcess they being
but little acquainted or effecting to be So.

_____ _____ _____

_____ _____ _____

_____ _____ _____

_____ _____ _____

_____ _____ _____

_____ _____ _____

Name _____

MARKING YOUR MAP

Cut apart the flags, glue them to toothpicks, and add them to your relief map.

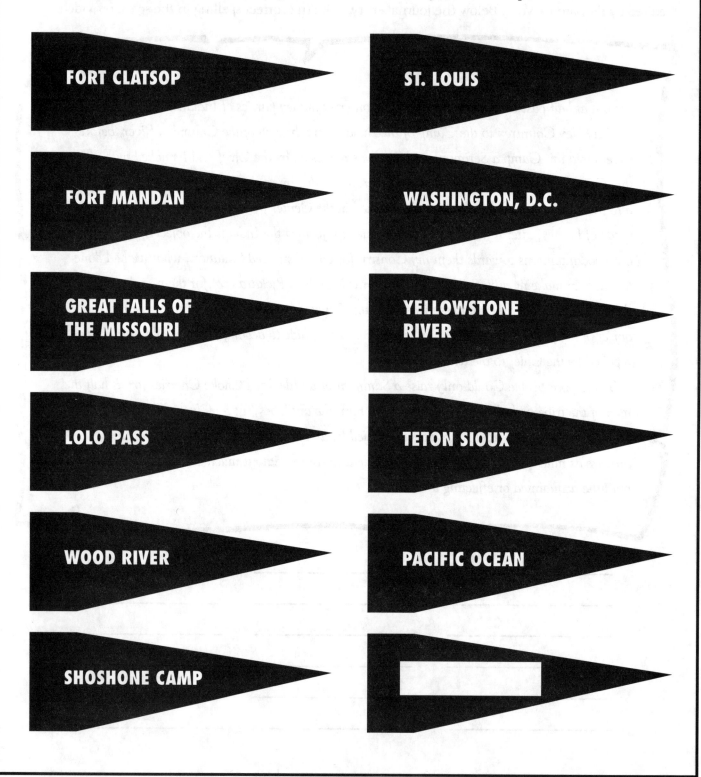

FORT CLATSOP

ST. LOUIS

FORT MANDAN

WASHINGTON, D.C.

GREAT FALLS OF
THE MISSOURI

YELLOWSTONE
RIVER

LOLO PASS

TETON SIOUX

WOOD RIVER

PACIFIC OCEAN

SHOSHONE CAMP

Name _____

DETAILED DESCRIPTIONS

Because cameras had not yet been invented in 1803, Captain Lewis had to describe unknown animals in a way that President Jefferson would understand. Try to describe the animals that Lewis saw (pictured below) to someone who has no idea what they look like.

Here's the beginning of a play based on Lewis and Clark's journals.
Your assignment is to finish it. Be creative and have fun. But remember:
The story must be based on what the explorers described in their journals.

Lewis and Clark's Excellent Adventure
Started by Justin Martin

Characters:

Narrator
Meriwether Lewis: Co-captain of the expedition;
  skilled in botany, zoology, and other sciences
William Clark: Other co-captain; skilled in
  navigation and communication with Indians
George Drouillard: Expedition's most skilled
  hunter and interpreter
Private Pierre Cruzatte: Crewman
Private Reuben Fields: Crewman
Private Silas Goodrich: Crewman

Characters you may want to add:

Toussaint Charbonneau: French-Canadian fur trader who served as an interpreter
Sacagawea: Shoshone woman; Charbonneau's wife
John Shields: Blacksmith

ACT 1, SCENE 1: 1804. A campsite beside the Missouri River
NARRATOR: In 1803, the United States purchased the Louisiana Territory from France.
The Louisiana Purchase added over 800,000 square miles of land to the United States.
The purchase more than doubled the size of the country. The area included all or part of 13
present-day states, such as Iowa, Kansas, and Missouri. In 1804, President Thomas Jefferson
sent Captains Meriwether Lewis and William Clark along with a crew of skilled boatmen,
hunters, and soldiers to explore the new territory. Their mission was to map the region,
observe the plants and wildlife, learn the customs of the Native Americans, and try to find
a river route from the Atlantic to the Pacific oceans.

We join the expedition now as they pitch camp on the banks of the Missouri River in
what is today South Dakota. The date is late September of 1804. After a long day traveling
on the river, the crew has gathered around the campfire to discuss the day's events.

CLARK (*working on his map as he speaks*): I estimate that we traveled 12 miles on the
Missouri today. Right here, at about the halfway point, Reuben Fields spotted a creek
flowing off to the east. We'll name it Reuben Creek in his honor. And about two miles
back, you may remember, we passed a small island in the river. A good day's travel—right?

CRUZATTE, FIELDS, and GOODRICH: Right!

CLARK: Everyone's in a good humor?

CRUZATTE, FIELDS, and GOODRICH: Right!

CLARK: Then we'll call this Good Humored Island.

LEWIS (*opening up his journal and preparing to take notes*):
What about wildlife? Did anyone spot any unusual animals today?

DROUILLARD: I hiked a little way inland and spotted a herd of buffalo. Didn't hit any. I got five elk, though. Looks like we're having elk for dinner tomorrow and the day after that—and the day after that.

FIELDS: I was walking in an open patch of land and I spotted a whole group of barking squirrels—funny little animals, standing on their hind legs and chattering. Must have been thousands of them.

CRUZATTE (*excitedly*): I saw this one critter! Like a beaver in shape and size; his head and mouth were like a dog; his—

LEWIS: Slow down, Peter.

CRUZATTE (*still excited*): His tail and hair were like those of a groundhog, but longer, and lighter colored. His skin was thick and loose. His belly was white and—uh–uh—he had a white streak running from his nose to his shoulders. I think he was some kind of small bear.

LEWIS: Sounds like the animal you saw might be what the French call a *brarrow*.

CLARK: Or what the Pawnee Indians call a *cho car tooch*.

LEWIS: Anyone else spot any unusual wildlife? What about you, Silas?

GOODRICH (*scratching himself*): Nothing but these pesky 'skeeters.

NARRATOR: The members of the Lewis and Clark expedition encountered many interesting animals that were unknown to them. The barking squirrels that Rueben Fields saw are what we now call prairie dogs. And the animal that got Pierre Cruzatte so excited was a badger.

Part 3

On the Trail

What Native American Groups Did Lewis and Clark Encounter?

In August of 1804, Lewis and Clark first met a group of Oto Indians. They invited leaders from the Otos and Missouri to their camp at Council Bluff, where they gave them medals, blankets, and coats. Lewis promised support from the "Great Father" (President Thomas Jefferson). In return the Otos warned them of the warring Teton Sioux upriver and of the ravages of smallpox, which had killed many in their village.

At the end of August, the expedition arrived at a Yankton Sioux camp. The Sioux greeted them warmly and invited the corps to a feast in their honor. Lewis again gave gifts and shared the message that the "Great Father" wanted peace. When the expedition met the Teton Sioux on September 23, 1804, Lewis gave a similar speech. Without the presence of their inter-preter, Drouillard, however, the Teton warriors could not understand Lewis. When presents were mistakenly presented to one chief and not another, conflict broke out. Clark was forced to draw his sword and the men were told to prepare to fight. Fortunately, Chief Black Buffalo inter-vened, and after spending several days with the Sioux, they were able to travel peaceably upriver again.

What Was Smallpox?

Smallpox was a virus that raged throughout Europe and America in the early 1800s. It was very deadly, and for reasons that are not fully understood, Indians were more susceptible to it than whites. Probably transmitted by French fur trappers who preceded the Lewis and Clark expedition, hundreds of thousands of Indians died from smallpox.

Beginning in the late 1700s, a vaccine was available that protected people against the dis-ease. To be inoculated, a person's skin was scratched until it bled. Then the vaccine was applied to the scratch. All members of the expedition were vaccinated before they departed. However, none of the Native Americans they encountered had access to the vaccine.

Where Did Lewis and Clark Spend the Winter in 1804-05?

Lewis and Clark spent the winter close to the Mandan and Minitari (Hidatsa) Indians. Just north of where Bismarck, North Dakota, is today, they built Fort Mandan, which consisted of eight log cabins surrounded by a log fence. During the winter, the men hunted, sewed clothes from hides, and made new dugout canoes. On Christmas, wrote Sergeant Ordway, we "fired the Swivels at day break & each man fired one round. Our Officers Gave the party a drink of Taffee, we had the Best to eat that could be had, & continued firing dancing & frolicking during the whole day."

At Fort Mandan, Lewis and Clark met Toussaint Charbonneau, a French-Canadian trapper, and his wife, Sacagawea. Charbonneau joined the expedition as an interpreter. In February, Sacagawea gave birth to a son, Jean Baptiste, in the fort.

In April, Lewis and Clark sent a crew back down the Missouri to St. Louis with specimens and notes for Jefferson. Among the items for the President were buffalo robes, red fox skins, a live prairie dog, four magpies, and a painted hide depicting the Sioux and Ricaras battling the Minnetrees and Mandans. Thirty-three members of the expedition continued upriver in two pirogues and six dugout canoes.

Who Was Sacagawea?

Sacagawea was the sixteen-year-old wife of Tousssaint Charbonneau. She met Lewis and Clark at Fort Mandan when they hired her husband as a guide and interpreter. Shoshone by birth, she was captured by the Hidatsa when

she was just ten. Sacagawea quickly came to help the crew by teaching them how to gather edible plants. She also acted as translator for Lewis and Clark several times west of the Rockies. Her presence as a wife and mother helped Indians realize that the expedition had come in peace, for no war party would travel with a woman and child.

What Were the Great Falls?

The Hidatsa told Lewis of the Great Falls on the Missouri (near present-day Great Falls, Montana). When he viewed the falls in June of 1805, Lewis wrote that they were one of the grandest sights he had ever seen. They also proved to be extremely difficult to maneuver around. It took the expedition three weeks to move their heavy canoes and gear 18 miles around the falls. To accomplish this, they made

Gifts Brought for Indians

- ✔ leggings
- ✔ garters
- ✔ coats
- ✔ blankets
- ✔ mirrors
- ✔ gunpowder
- ✔ whiskey
- ✔ beads
- ✔ tobacco
- ✔ knives
- ✔ bells
- ✔ medals
- ✔ certificates of merit
- ✔ belts
- ✔ pipes
- ✔ silk scarves
- ✔ United States flags

some crude wagons from cottonwood trees, piled up their canoes and supplies, and pushed and pulled the wagons overland. It was difficult trekking where there were no trails, and the men frequently complained of prickly pear cactus spines cutting through their moccasins.

STUDENT ACTIVITIES

FOOD FOR AN EXPEDITION

Lewis and Clark relied on skilled hunters and trappers to supply most of their food. In addition to fish, they ate a lot of wild game meat, including buffalo, deer, bear, and antelope. To supple-ment their diet, Sacagawea gathered plants such as camas root, chokecherries, and rosehips.

When they shared meals with Indians along their route, the explorers feasted on many traditional Native American foods. Using the recipes below, make and sample some dishes that are similar to those Lewis and Clark tasted on their journey. (Note: Some of the ingredients have been modified for easier preparation.)

Pemmican

Pemmican was a traditional Indian food made with dried meat, berries, and seeds mixed with fat. It was often eaten in the winter when fresh meat and fruit were scarce.

Some of the Indian Tribes Lewis and Clark Met

Common Name Today	What They Call Themselves
Arikara	Tanish
Atsina (Gros Ventre)	Naaninin
Blackfoot (Piegan/Blood)	Siksika
Crow	Absaroka
Dakota (Santee)	Isanyati
Hidatsa (Minitaree/Gros Ventre)	Absaroka
Lakota (Teton Sioux)	Titonwan
Mandan	Numakaki
Minnetarees	
Missouri	
Nakota (Yankton Sioux)	Ihunktonwan
Omaha	Omaha
Osage	Niuko'nska
Otos	
Pawnee (Skidi)	Chahiksichahiks
Nez Percé	Ne Mee Poo
Salish (Flathead)	Salish
Shoshone	
Yakama	Waptailimim
Chinook (Clatsop)	
Tillamook	
Walla Walla	

INGREDIENTS

- ✔ 1 cup of hulled sunflower seeds
- ✔ 1 cup of beef jerky (cut into small pieces)
- ✔ 1 cup of raisins or currants

DIRECTIONS

1. Blend all ingredients together in a food processor. Store in an airtight container.

2. Before serving, discuss with students how Native Americans made pemmican from dried buffalo, camas root, chokecherries, and roasted seeds that were ground together using stones and mixed with fat.

3. Before serving, go over all substituted ingredients with the class to make sure no one has a related food allergy. When serving, place a teaspoon of the pemmican in each student's hand to taste and enjoy.

Frybread

Traditionally, Plains Indians ground seeds, roots, or corn into a flour that was mixed with water and cooked or fried in buffalo fat.

INGREDIENTS

- ✔ 1 1/2 to 2 cups warm water
- ✔ 3 cups all-purpose flour
- ✔ 1 tablespoon baking powder
- ✔ 2 cups vegetable oil for frying
- ✔ Paper towels

DIRECTIONS

1. Blend the flour, baking powder, and water together until the mixture forms a soft, but not sticky, dough. Knead for several minutes. Then let the dough sit for about ten minutes more.

2. Pour oil in a deep skillet until it is one-inch deep. Heat the oil and drop in small egg-size pieces of dough that have been flattened. Fry the rounds for three to five minutes until browned.

3. Drain on paper towels and serve immediately.

Berry Soup

In the early 1800s, Plains Indians would have made berry soup in an animal-skin pouch using hot rocks to keep it warm.

INGREDIENTS

- ✔ 4 cups of fresh or frozen blueberries or blackberries
- ✔ 1/2 cup honey
- ✔ 1/4 cup cornstarch

DIRECTIONS

1. Place the berries in a large pot and cover with water. Boil for five minutes and then simmer.

2. Stir the honey and cornstarch into the hot berries. Cook the soup for a few minutes until it thickens.

3. Pour into bowls and serve with frybread.

INDIAN GROUPS

Lewis and Clark encountered many Indian groups during their journey. (See the chart on page 34.) Each spoke a different language and observed its own social, religious, and political

customs. While some Indians such as the Otos, Mandans, Nez Percé, and Shoshone, welcomed the expedition, others, such as the Teton Sioux and Blackfeet, were wary. Encourage students to learn more about these Native American cultures by reading the Lewis and Clark journals and researching the groups in encyclopedias and other reference books. Invite students to work in pairs to prepare a short report about one group to share with the rest of the class.

MATERIAL WORLD

Indians traditionally used plant and animal resources to create everyday items. For example, bison and elk were a resource for food, clothing, containers, needles, and thread. Wood was used for tipi poles, travois frames, and pipe stems. Stone, such as obsidian and chert, was used for knives and points. Quills, animal hair, feathers, bones, teeth, and claws were used to decorate jewelry. Although Indians continued to value these natural resources, over the years, they also sought many of the new materials that were brought by early explorers. For example, wool was useful for clothing. Metal was prized for

tools, and glass beads were popular for decorating clothing and other household items.

As you start your discussions of this section, have students distinguish between the natural resources Indians used and the goods they received from early explorers.

Members of the Corps of Discovery brought and acquired a tremendous number of items on their trek west. Some they gave to Indians as gifts. Other things were given to them by Indians or obtained along the way. Using the reproducible on page 38, invite students to identify each object and determine which ones were probably gifts to Indians and which ones were most likely given to the crew during the course of their journey. (See page 64 for answers.)

SPEAKING THROUGH SIGN LANGUAGE

Different Indian groups often used sign language to communicate with one another. When he could not understand their words, Drouillard used sign language with Indians and interpreted the hand motions for Lewis and Clark. Copy the reproducible on page 39 and let students experiment with sign language. Then have the class play a game of "charades." To start, invite one student to compose a sentence and try to communicate it to the rest of the class using sign language. The student who interprets the hand signals correctly then takes a turn in front of the class.

HISTORICAL PERSPECTIVES

We know a lot about how Lewis and Clark viewed their adventure because their journals have been published. But we know much less about the expedition from the Indians' point of view. Many of their stories and drawings have never circulated beyond the Indian population. In this activity, challenge students to think about what it must have meant for a Native American to have met Lewis and Clark at a time when some Indian groups in the West had yet to see a white person.

MATERIALS
✔ reproducible pages 40 and 41
✔ markers or crayons

DIRECTIONS
1. Invite a student to read the journal entry on the reproducible aloud.

2. Ask students to imagine how these Indians might have felt about seeing the Corps of Discovery. What might they have talked about? How might they have recorded the event from their perspective? Invite students to draw a series of pictures that could describe the event from the Indians' point of view.

FINDING THEIR WAY
Sometimes, it was not clear in which direction the expedition should go. For example, in June of 1805, the travelers came to a place on the Missouri where the river divided into two smaller bodies of water. The explorers asked themselves, "Which way should we go?" Use the scenario cards on pages 42 and 43 and have the class decide the best route to take.

MATERIALS
✔ six copies of "River Mystery" cards found on pages 42 and 43

DIRECTIONS
1. Before you begin, cut apart the six copies of the "River Mystery" cards along the dotted lines. Then match up the cards, place each matched pair type sides out, and staple them closed. Keep the cards together in a set.

2. Divide your students into six teams (or more or less as necessary). Hand each team a set of "River Mystery" cards. Tell them to read each card in order from 1 to 5. The cards will tell each team what to do.

3. Give students half an hour to discuss the information on the cards. When they are finished, have each team share the route they chose to follow.

4. Discuss how their choices compare with the route that the expedition chose.

False Expectations

◆ A massive 180-mile-long "Mountain of Salt" was thought to exist in the West.

◆ Legend held that a group of Welsh people lived in the mountains and still carried Welsh royal treasures with them.

◆ Giants were rumored to exist, as was a tribe of pygmies.

◆ Some thought the expedition would encounter wild llamas.

◆ Mammoths were thought to still thrive in the wilds.

WHO HAS WHAT?

Write the name of each object in the space provided using the list below.

  Place a star next to all objects that corps members brought with them.

  Place an X next to all objects that Lewis and Clark either gave to the Indians as gifts or used as trade goods.

  Place a circle next to all objects that the Indians gave in return or traded.

1.

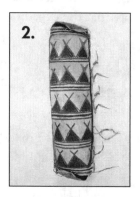
2.

3.

4.

_____ _____ _____ _____

5.

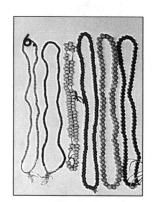
6.

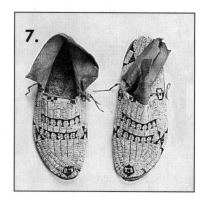
7.

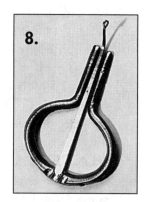
8.

_____ _____ _____ _____

Objects

voyageur's touke	glass beads	folk harp	buffalo robe
peace medal	moccasins	bonnet case	fire starter

Answer the questions below on the back of this page.

1. Why did Lewis and Clark bring gifts to the Indians?
2. What goods or supplies did they use for trading?
3. What items did Lewis and Clark hope to obtain?
4. What do you think were the most valuable trade goods that Lewis and Clark carried?
   Give reasons for your choices.
5. Do you think there was anything that Lewis and Clark would not trade?

SIGN LANGUAGE

Indian groups traditionally used sign language to communicate with one another. Lewis and Clark's interpreter, Drouillard, also used hand signals to help him better understand Indian languages.
Practice some of the signs below. Then try them out on friends. Can they guess what you are trying to say?

hunger   lightning   many   moon   mountain

peace   rain   see   snake   sun

talk   tree   brothers   come   deer

eat   fire   grass   hear   heart

Name _____

HISTORICAL PERSPECTIVE

Read the following journal entry reprinted from *The Journals of the Lewis and Clark Expedition*, Volume 5, edited by Gary E. Moulton. On the back side of this sheet of paper, draw a picture—from the Indian's perspective—of their interaction with the Corps of Discovery on the Columbia River.

(Clark) October 19th 1805

I observed a great number of Lodges on the opposit Side at Some distance below, and Several Indians on the opposit bank passing up to where Capt. Lewis was with the Canoes, others I Saw on a knob nearly opposit to me at which place they delayed but a Short time, before they returned to their Lodges as fast as they could run, I was fearfull that those people might not be informed of us, deturmined to take the little Canoe which was with me and proceed with the three men in it to the Lodges, on my aproach not one person was to be seen except three men off in the plains, and they Sheared off as I saw approached near the Shore, I landed in front of five Lodges which was at no great distance from each other, Saw no person the enterance or Dores of the Lodges wer Shut with the Same materials of which they were built a mat, I approached one with a pipe in my hand entered a lodge which was the nearest to me found 32 persons men, women, and a few children Setting permicuesly in the Lodg, in the greatest agutation, Some crying and ringing there hands, others hanging their heads. I gave my hand to them all and made Signs of my friendly dispotion and offered the men my pipe to Smok and distributed a fiew Small articles which I had in my pockets, this measure passified those distressed people verry much, I then Sent one man into each lodge and entered a Second myself the inhabitants of which I found more fritened than those of the first lodge I destributed Sundrey Small articles amongst them, and Smoked with the men, I then entered the third 4h & fifth Lodge which I found Somewhat passified, the three men , Drewer Jo. & R. Fields haveing useed everey means in their power to convience them of our friendly disposition to them, I then Set my Self on a rock and made Signs to the men to come and Smoke with me not one Come out untill the Canoes arrived with the 2 chiefs, one of whom spoke aloud, and as was their Custom to all we had passed the Indians came out & Set by me and Smoked They said we came from the clouds &c &c. and were not men &c. &c. this time Capt. Lewis came down with the Canoes rear in which the Indian, as Soon as they Saw the Squar wife of the interperters they pointed to her and informed those who continued iyet the Same position I first found them they imediately all came out and appeared to assume new life the sight of This Indian woman, wife to one of our interprs. confirmed those people of our friendly intentions, as no woman ever accompanies a war party of Indians in this quarter.

—reprinted by permission of the University of Nebraska Press.

Name _____

Use your imagination and the information from the journal entry to create a hide painting of the events that occurred on October 19, 1805. Your drawing should be from the point of view of the Indians.

FINDING THEIR WAY

River Mystery Card # 1

To play "River Mystery," read the instructions on each card. Do not look at any other cards until you have finished each task. You may now open Card #2.

River Mystery Card #2

In June 1805, the expedition came to a place where the Missouri River divided into two small bodies of water, both the same size. The north fork of the river was muddy—just like the Missouri. The south fork was clear and lined with rocks. Based on this information, determine which route the explorers should take. Decide as a group and then pick up Card #3.

River Mystery Card #3

The corps believed that the northern route was best, but Lewis and Clark were not convinced. They decided to split up and explore each stream farther. Lewis and some men walked along the north fork; Clark headed south. The southern stream looked as if it flowed into the mountains and disappeared; the northern one resembled a river described by the Indians. Which way would you go? (When the group agrees, open Card #4.)

River Mystery Card #4

When Lewis and Clark reunited the corps, everyone was convinced that the north fork was the best route to take. But Lewis was still uncertain. What would you do as the leader of the expedition? (When the group agrees, open Card #5.)

River Mystery Card #5

Lewis decided to take a group of men to explore the south fork of the river. They walked until they saw the Great Falls of the Missouri. They were on the right track. They went back, got their canoes, and proceeded on. The water in the south fork was clear and full of rocks—like most streams coming down the mountains. It led them to the headwaters of the Missouri. Remember that headwaters are the small streams that are the sources of a river.

FINDING THEIR WAY

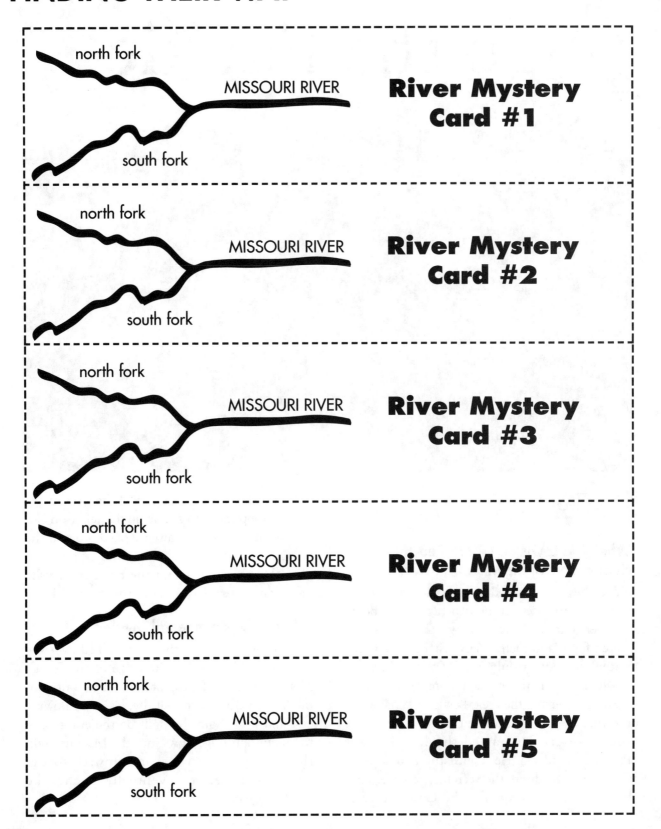

River Mystery Card #1

River Mystery Card #2

River Mystery Card #3

River Mystery Card #4

River Mystery Card #5

Part 4

To the Pacific

When Did Lewis and Clark Reach the Headwaters of the Missouri River?

Once they maneuvered around the Great Falls, the expedition continued to take their boats upriver. Clark chose to leave the corps and search for a land route. Clark reached the headwaters on foot on July 25, 1805. On July 27, Lewis and his men met them there by boat.

After surveying the area, Lewis gave names to the three rivers that formed the headwaters of the Missouri. He named the largest after President Jefferson. He named the middle river after James Madison, the secretary of state. And he called the east branch the Gallatin, after

Albert Gallatin, the secretary of the treasury.

The group traveled a mile up the Jefferson and set up camp. As Sacagawea looked around, she recognized that this was the land of her people—the Shoshone—and the place where she had been captured as an eleven-year-old girl.

What Is the Continental Divide?

On August 12, 1805, the men walked over the continental divide, or the ridge of the Rocky Mountains. Like the top of a roof, the continental divide is the place that divides water flowing east and west. Rain that falls on the east side of the mountain ridge flows into the Missouri; rain that falls on the west side flows into the Columbia River and eventually reaches the Pacific Ocean.

How Did the Expedition Travel on Land?

Lewis and Clark knew they needed to find horses to make the difficult trek over the mountains. They hoped that the Shoshone might help.

When they arrived at the Indian camp, Sacagawea found that her brother was now the Shoshone chief. Acting as a translator, she persuaded him to help the explorers cross the Rockies. The crew acquired 29 horses in exchange for clothing, knives, and guns. Then they sank their canoes, stored some of their supplies, and began the arduous trek overland.

How Did the Corps Get Over the Rockies?

In September of 1805, Lewis and Clark led the men over the Bitterroot Mountains, a range of the Rockies. It was already winter. Falling snow made the ground slick and there was little to eat. To survive, they had to eat one of their horses, the candles they made out of bear fat, and some of the tasteless soup that Lewis had brought in canisters.

On the other side of the Rockies, they met the Nez Percé. These friendly Indians gave the starving corps salmon, berries, and bread made of root flour. After some much-needed rest, the men began making canoes the Nez Percé way, by burning out logs. Lewis branded their horses, which they left with the Nez Percé, and started down the Clearwater, Snake, and Columbia rivers.

When Did the Expedition Reach the Ocean?

In November of 1805, the men reached "the great Pacific Ocean which we been so long anxious to See." They constructed Fort Clatsop near present-day Astoria, Oregon, to stay for the winter. It was named after the local Clatsop Indians.

What Was Life Like at Fort Clatsop?

The winter of 1805-06 proved to be difficult for the explorers. It rained almost every day and the men were constantly wet and cold. They spent a lot of time inside the fort. While Lewis and Clark worked on their journals and maps and traded with neighboring Indian groups for supplies, the men made clothes from hides. Some of the crew ventured out to find food, while others were sent to boil down ocean water to get salt. One time, they went to the beach to see the remains of a whale that had been killed by Indians. Lewis and Clark traded their goods for 300 pounds of whale blubber that they used for cooking.

How Did Lewis and Clark Return Home?

After a difficult and gloomy winter at Fort Clatsop, the expedition was eager to return home. They left in March and started upstream on the Columbia River. They visited the Walla Walla Indians, whom they had met heading west, and then spent a month with the Nez Percé. As they waited for the snow to melt in the mountains, Clark opened up an infirmary to treat sick Indians in exchange for much-needed food. Once over the Rockies, Lewis and Clark split the corps into two groups so they could explore more territory before reaching the Missouri River. Lewis went back to see the headwaters of the Marias River; Clark headed south to explore and map the Yellowstone River.

Lewis's party returned to the cache of supplies that they had left south of the Great Falls. Then they entered Blackfeet country to see the Marias. When a group of Indians tried to steal some of his horses, Lewis shot and killed a man. It was the only time the corps had killed anyone on the journey. Shortly thereafter, Lewis was also shot. Private Cruzatte shot him in the buttocks, mistakenly thinking that the explorer was an elk.

Clark's return route took the crew through the Gallatin Valley of Montana and down along the Yellowstone River.

The two leaders finally reunited on the Missouri and, after a quick trip downstream in their canoes, reached the Mandan villages. Charbonneau and Sacagawea returned to their home. Charbonneau was paid $500 for helping the expedition.

Expedition Medicines

While the Corps of Discovery was exposed to many diseases and suffered injuries and illnesses, only one member died during the trip. This outcome is credited to Lewis and Clark's excellent leadership skills and conscientious medical care. Along the way, they treated many Indians, as well.

Invite students to compare the illnesses below to the best treatment known at the time of Lewis and Clark.

Illness	Treatment
Headache	Drink tea made from Peruvian bark.
Snakebite	Apply a poultice made of gunpowder and Peruvian bark.
Dysentery or Diarrhea	Swallow some of Dr. Rush's bilious diarrhea pills (a laxative made of jalap and calomel).
Abdominal pain or fever	Bloodletting (making a cut to bleed out the bad blood)
Intestinal cramps	Drink chokecherry tea.

The entire crew arrived in St. Louis on September 23, 1806, after traveling almost 8,000 miles in two years, four months, and nine days. What an adventure it had been!

Clothes for an Expedition

Lewis and Clark started their journey wearing European-style clothing and hard-soled leather shoes. These clothes quickly wore out. By the time the men reached the Shoshone, they had on hide clothes like the Indians. The Mandan taught them how to tan elk and buffalo hides using animal brains, how to sew leather together using sinew (dried animal tendons), and how to make moccasins. These hide clothes proved to be warmer and more waterproof than European-style cloth garments.

Fun Facts

◆ In 1806, William Clark wrote in his journal of finding huge rib bones in some Montana rocks, which he attributed to fish. More than likely, they were dinosaur bones.

◆ Lewis and Clark never did find the famed Welsh people that were rumored to live in the Rocky Mountains.

A DAY IN THE LIFE OF LEWIS

Captain Lewis's journal entry on June 14, 1805, documents a hair-raising day of adventures in the Rocky Mountains. Have students outline the day based on Lewis's journal. To help them get started, reproduce the student activity found on page 50.

OVER THE CONTINENTAL DIVIDE

To show your students how water flows in opposite directions off the continental divide, try this simple demonstration using your relief map.

MATERIALS
✔ relief map
✔ 1 cup of water

DIRECTIONS

1. Gather students around the relief map. Remind them that Lewis and Clark traveled upstream (against the current) on the Missouri River heading west, and downstream (with the current) on the Snake and Columbia rivers. Review the major river systems that flow off the Rocky Mountains. On their return trip, the corps traveled upstream on which river? On which river did they travel downstream?

2. Pour a little water on your relief map over the Rocky Mountains. When it rains in the Rockies, where does the water flow? Look carefully at the rivets coming off the map. The continental divide, running along the spine of the mountains, provides the clue. Water coming off the eastern side of the mountains flows into the Missouri River, then into the Mississippi, and eventually into the Atlantic Ocean. Water flowing off the west-

ern side of the Rockies flows into the Snake River, then into the Columbia, and finally into the Pacific Ocean.

WINTER AT FORT CLATSOP

Lewis and Clark described the winter of 1805–06 at Fort Clatsop as wet and miserable, but also busy. To help students better understand the corps' experience there, read aloud some of Lewis and Clark's journal entries at the fort. Then encourage students to assume the role of an expedition member who is writing a letter home to his family. The letter should describe what life was like at Fort Clatsop.

MAKING SALT

Salt was greatly valued by the corps. It helped food taste better during the long winter spent at Fort Clatsop. To obtain salt, the men boiled down seawater in kettles and then scraped up the remaining salt. Your students should enjoy trying this procedure themselves.

MATERIALS

✔ pan
✔ 1 cup water
✔ 1/2 cup salt
✔ hot plate
✔ pot holder

DIRECTIONS

1. Dissolve the salt in a pan full of water. Put the pan on the hot plate and bring the water to a boil. Let the water boil away.

2. Let the pan cool thoroughly and then pass it around to show students what remains after salt water is boiled away. Discuss how much salt the corps collected. How much time do you think the men spent collecting salt? Have students consult the journals to find out.

IN THE NEWS

After 2 years, 4 months, 12 days, and thousands of miles, the expedition safely returned to St.

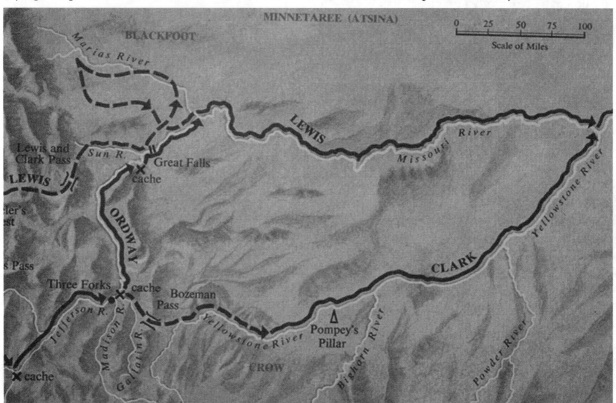

Louis on September 23, 1806. By now, most Americans had given the men up for dead. What would the headline story be in the *Washington Times*, the newspaper in the nation's capital? Copy the reproducible on page 51, pass it out, and let your class decide.

EXPEDITION CHALLENGE

Use the reproducible on page 52 to assess how students are mastering the major events of the expedition. Look to see how well they put the activities of Lewis and Clark in chronological order. (Answers are on page 64.)

SUPER JOURNAL CHALLENGE

To see who has really been paying attention, read aloud the following journal entries from *The Journals of Lewis and Clark*, edited by Bernard DeVoto. See who can guess where the expedition is based on these entries. Anyone who answers correctly is an honorary member of the corps!

(Lewis)
August 19, 1805
The Shoshonees may be estimated at about 100 warriors, and about three times that number of women and children. They have more children among them than I expected to have seen among a people who procure subsistence with such difficulty.
(The headwaters of the Missouri)

(Lewis)
January, 29, 1806
Nothing worthy of notice occurred today. our fare is the flesh of lean elk boiled with pure water, and a little salt. The whale blubber which we have used very sparingly is now exhausted. On this food I do not feel strong, but enjoy the most perfect health.
(Fort Clatsop)

(Clark)
January 27, 1805
attempt to Cut our Boat and Canoos out of the ice, a deficuelt Task I fear as we find water between the Ice, I bleed the man with the Plurisy to day & Swet him, Capt. Lewis took off the Toes of one foot of the Boy eho got frost bit Some time ago.
(Fort Mandan)

(Lewis)
July 30, 1805
Capt. Clark being much better this morning and having completed my observations we reloaded our canoes and set out, assending Jeffersons river. Shabono, his woman two invalleds and myself walked through the bottom ob the Lard side of the river about 4 1/2 miles when we again struck it at the place the woman informed us she was taken prisoner.
(The headwaters of the Missouri)

(Clark)
October 17, 1805
Those people appear of a mild disposition and friendly disposed. They have in their huts independant of their nets gigs & fishing tackling each bows & large quivers or arrows on which they use flint Spikes.
(The Snake River)

(Lewis)
June 3, 1805
we took the width of the two rivers, found the left hand or S. fort 372 yards and the N. fork 200. The noth fork is deeper than the other but it's courant not so swift; it's waters run in the same boiling and roling manner which has uniformly characterized the Missouri throughout it's whole course so far.
(The junction of the Marias and Missouri rivers)

Excerpts reprinted by permission of the Houghton Mifflin Company.

A DAY IN THE LIFE OF CAPTAIN LEWIS

June 14, 1805, was an amazing day for Captain Lewis. First, read the journal entry. Then make a list of all the things that happened to Lewis on that day.

(Lewis) June 14, 1805

I scelected a fat buffaloe and shot him very well, through the lungs; while I was gazeing attentively on the poor animal discharging blood in streams from his mouth and nostrils, expecting him to fall every instant, and having entirely forgotten to reload my rifle, a large white, or reather brown bear, had perceived and crept on me within 20 steps before I discovered him; in the first moment I drew up my gun to shoot, but at the same instant recolected that she was not loaded and that he was too near for me to hope to perform this opperation before he reached me, as he was then briskly advancing on me….in this situation I thought of retreating in a brisk walk as fast as he was advancing untill I could reach a tree about 300 yards below me, but I had no sooner terned myself about but he pitched at me, open mouthed and full speed, I ran fast about 80 yards and found he gained on me fast, I then run into the water….at this instant he arrived at the edge of the water within about 20 feet of me; the moment I put myself in this attitude of defence he sudonly wheeled about as if frightened….As soon as I saw him run in that manner I returned to the shore and charged my gun, which I had still retained in my hand throughout this curious adventure….in returning through the level bottom of the Medecine river and about 200 yards distant from the Missouri, my direction led me directly to an anamal that I first supposed was a wolf; but on nearer approach or about sixty paces distant I discovered it was not it's colour was a brownish yellow…I took aim at it and fired…I loaded my gun and examined the place which was dusty and saw the track from which I am still further convinced that it was of the tiger kind…I had not proceeded more than three hundred yards from the burrow of this tyger cat, before three bull buffaloe, which wer feeding with a large herd about half a mile from me on my left, seperated from the herd and ran full speed toward me. I thought at least to give them some amusement and altered my direction…I then continued my rout homewards passed the buffaloe which I had killed, but did not think it prudent to remain all night at this place.

From *The Journals of Lewis and Clark* edited by Bernard DeVoto and reprinted by permission of the Houghton Mifflin Company.

Use the other side of this sheet to make a list of all of the things that happened to Captain Lewis on June 14, 1805. Then answer the questions below.

1. How many animals did Lewis see that day?

2. How many shots did he fire?

3. How many bullets could be loaded in his gun at any one time?

4. Do you think that Lewis was ever scared?

Name _____

IN THE NEWS

Write the front-page story following the return of the Lewis and Clark expedition to St. Louis. Be sure to include details about their journey.

Washington Times

| VOL. MII | SEPTEMBER 1806 | NO. 36 |

_____   _____

_____   _____

_____   _____

_____   _____

_____   _____

_____   _____

_____   _____

_____   _____

_____   _____

Name _____

EXPEDITION CHALLENGE

The adventures of Lewis and Clark listed below are not in the correct order. Cut apart this page on the dotted lines and see if you can put the events in the order in which they occurred.

The expedition floats down the Columbia River.

Lewis and Clark obtain horses from the Shoshone and travel overland in search of the Columbia River.

Lewis and Clark arrive at the headwaters of the Missouri.

The explorers carry their boats and supplies around the Great Falls of the Missouri.

Lewis and Clark build Fort Mandan for use as a winter camp.

The crew goes over the Rocky Mountains at Lolo Pass.

The crew begins traveling up the Missouri River.

Lewis and Clark divide the party: Lewis explores other routes to the Great Falls; Clark explores the Yellowstone River.

The United States buys the Louisiana Territory from France.

The crew reunites and arrives in St. Louis.

The expedition reaches the Pacific Ocean.

Lewis and Clark confront the Teton Sioux and continue up the river.

Lewis and Clark establish camp on the Wood River in Illinois.

The explorers build Fort Clatsop as a winter camp.

Part 5

Retracing Their Steps

BACKGROUND INFORMATION

What Happened to Lewis and Clark?

After the expedition, Meriwether Lewis was named governor of the Louisiana Territory. However, he suffered from depression and on October 11, 1809, he was found dead of a gunshot wound. Historians believe that Lewis committed suicide. Clark, on the other hand, lived a long and productive life. He married, had a family, and served as governor of the Louisiana Territory after Lewis died. Clark made sure that all his notes and maps, as well as everything that Lewis had written, were published as President Jefferson had requested. As a reward for a successful journey, each expedition member was given 320 acres of land from the government upon his return, plus wages. Lewis and Clark received 1,600 acres each.

Can All the Places Where Lewis and Clark Went Be Identified?

Many of the places where Lewis and Clark traveled and established forts have been identified from notes in their journals. However, because it is difficult to mark the exact spot where they camped, site markers have been placed in the general vicinity. For example, even though Lewis and Clark spent over 800 nights in the

West and made more than 600 campsites, remains that could be linked directly to the explorers have never been found. That's where historical archaeologists come in.

Historical archaeologist Ken Karsmizki is searching for one of Lewis and Clark's campsites, a place where they spent nearly two weeks. This site, the Lower Portage Camp, was located just below the Great Falls on the Missouri River. Karsmizki knows from the journals the general vicinity of the camp. Now he is using archaeological techniques to find the exact site. But this type of archaeology can be slow and often frustrating because so many people have camped there over the last 2,000 years.

To date, Karsmizki has found a stake, bison bones, and evidence of cooking hearths that were left at the site near the year 1810 (plus or minus ten years). But he has not found a single artifact that clearly links the spot to Lewis and Clark.

What Lewis and Clark Artifacts Could Be Found?

Potentially, there are many different artifacts that could be found, such as peace medals, tent poles, beads, buttons, canisters, canoes, cooking pots, stakes, even Lewis's iron boat. But because so many people have passed through the same area, it's difficult, though not impossible, to link any of these objects directly to the Lewis and Clark expedition. One method is to scientifically date artifacts using radiocarbon dating techniques.

How Can These Artifacts Be Dated?

Artifacts that are thought to belong to Lewis and Clark can be dated by measuring the amount of carbon 14 that remains. This "radiocarbon" dating technique works only on organic materials, such as wood. Since carbon 14 decays at a steady rate, archaeologists can tell the age of an object by determining how much carbon 14 remains.

The stake that Ken Karsmizki uncovered could be dated since it contains wood, one of the best materials for radiocarbon dating. Karsmizki determined that it was made around 1810, so it could have been used by the expedition. Although charcoal from fires can also be dated, measuring carbon 14 will not reveal when the fire was made. Rather, it shows the age of the wood that was burned.

Is Anyone Studying Lewis and Clark's Journals Today?

Historians are still studying the journals and maps of Lewis and Clark, as well as materials written by other crew members. Dr. Gary Moulton, a professor of history at the University of Nebraska at Lincoln, is in the process of editing the journals. He is currently on his fourteenth volume of notes about the expedition! Dr. Moulton started by collecting all known journal entries and maps and all research articles on Lewis and Clark's journey. Then, working with historians, ethnographers, and scientists, he put the journals and maps together in their proper sequence and added footnotes pertaining to important research done by other Lewis and Clark scholars. The published journals edited by Dr. Moulton make it easier for scholars and history buffs alike to learn more about the incredible adventures of Lewis and Clark.

STUDENT ACTIVITIES

PAINTING THE WEST

Surprisingly, Lewis and Clark did not take an illustrator with them. But less than 30 years later, the German explorer and botanist Prince Maximillian traveled up the Missouri accompanied by Karl Bodmer, a Swiss-born artist. Bodmer visited many of the same Indian groups that Lewis and Clark had met and sketched their portraits. Later, he painted over his sketches using watercolors. As many of these Indians were later decimated by smallpox, his art is one of the few remaining visual records of these people prior to the non-Indian settlement of the West. To share Bodmer's art with students and help them explore their own creative processes, copy the reproducible on page 58 and get artistic!

MATERIALS

✔ copies of the reproducible found on page 58
✔ watercolor paints
✔ paintbrushes
✔ paper cups (with a little water in the bottom)

DIRECTIONS

1. Before starting, have students discuss what they notice about the artwork. What are the Indians wearing? Could any of these items be linked to Lewis and Clark? Discuss what colors might be appropriate for the clothing and skin tones of the Indians.

2. Invite students to start painting their sketches using the watercolors. When they are finished, let the paintings dry and hang them up around your classroom.

WHAT IS AN ARTIFACT?

An artifact is any object made or used by humans. To help students distinguish artifacts from other specimens such as fossils, plants, animals, or rocks, try this simple classification activity.

MATERIALS

✔ 5 copies of the reproducible on page 59
✔ 5 paper clips
✔ 5 rocks
✔ 5 pencils
✔ 5 leaves
✔ 5 sticks
✔ 5 raisins
✔ 5 pennies

DIRECTIONS

1. Divide your class into five groups. Have one person from each group collect a copy of the handout, a paper clip, a rock, a pencil, a leaf, a stick, a raisin, and a penny.

2. Review with students the definition of an artifact. Then challenge each group of students to divide the objects into two piles: Those that are artifacts and those that are not. Once they have divided the objects, have them decide whether the wooden stake pictured on the handout is an artifact. Give them a few minutes to decide.

3. Discuss your students' conclusions. Which of these objects is an artifact? (Answer: Paper clips, pencils, raisins, and pennies are artifacts. Rocks, leaves, and sticks are not.) Why are raisins artifacts? Is the stake an artifact? Why? (The stake is an artifact because it was cut and shaped by humans. Lewis and Clark write in their journals about making stakes to tie down their tents and hold up their meat racks.)

GRIDDING A SITE

Before historical archaeologists begin to dig at any site, they must first divide the area into one-meter plots using the Cartesian coordinate system. This is done so they can accurately record the location of any artifacts they uncover. To introduce students to site gridding try this activity.

MATERIALS

- ✔ reproducibles on pages 60 and 61 (1 copy of page 60 for each student, and 2 copies of page 61)
- ✔ rulers
- ✔ pencils

DIRECTIONS

1. Discuss with students why it is important that archaeologists grid a site before they start digging. Then pass out copies of the Lower Portage Camp Site (page 60) and have students draw lines at every inch on both the horizontal and vertical axis. (See page 64 for the finished product.)

2. Once the grid lines are drawn, have students number each grid unit. Point out the "site datum" in the lower-left-hand corner and explain that it is the point from which the grid is established. The numbers start at the site datum point. That grid-unit number is 0,0. The unit directly above it is 0,1, the next is 0,2, and so on. The grid unit to the right of the site datum point is 1,0, the next is 2,0, and so on. Have students label each point on the grid.

3. Once they have labeled all the grid units on their site map, have them complete the chart on page 61.

SITE STRATIGRAPHY

At a site being dug by archeologists, objects closest to the surface are generally the newest and were left most recently. Older artifacts are found farther down in the ground. This site rule, called the *Law of Superposition*, is always true unless the site has been disturbed.

To show students how to date artifacts using the Law of Superposition, reproduce the handout on page 62 and begin.

PROTECTING LEWIS AND CLARK SITES

Vandalism at archaeological digs destroys the site itself as well as the potential to collect scientific information there. To help protect these valuable sites, the Archaeological Resources Protection Act was passed in 1979. This law makes it illegal to deface, injure, or collect material on public lands from any site more than 100 years old. To introduce students to some of the ethical issues dealing with artifacts and archaeological sites, have a student read aloud one of the following scenarios and discuss it with the class.

Scenario One

You are an amateur archaeologist. Near your town, the construction of a new dam will soon cover up several places where Lewis and Clark once camped. One of your friends invites you to go out to the sites and dig up a few artifacts. The dam will just cover them with water, she argues. What should you do?

Scenario Two

You are hiking along a trail at the Fort Clatsop National Monument. Suddenly, you notice something shiny on the ground and realize it's a strand of old beads. They are selling just one of these very beads for $100 at a shop in town. There are almost 200 beads on this string. What do you do? Should you pick it up even if you plan to give it to a park ranger?

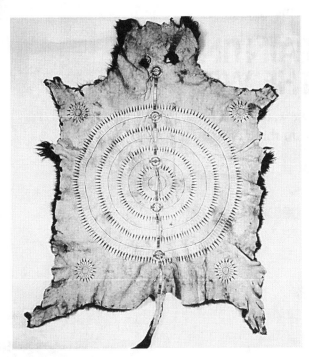

Scenario Three

You think that one of your best friends is digging up and selling Lewis and Clark artifacts. When you confront him, he says that he was digging on private land. Now you think he is lying. Should you follow him to catch him in the act? Should you call anyone? Can you ignore it?

STUDYING THEIR JOURNALS

Review the purpose of journal footnotes. Why do historians add them? Once students are familiar with the purpose of the footnotes, including those in the journals of Lewis and Clark, invite them to add a few of their own.

To start, have students pick a favorite journal entry and copy it on a sheet of paper. Do they have any questions about that particular day based on what the entry says? Do journal entries tell everything that happened?

Send students to the library or give them time to use the books in your classroom to learn more about what the expedition was doing at that point in time. Then have students write some notes that add to the information that the journal entry already provides.

Name _____

PAINTING THE WEST

Use watercolors to
paint this drawing.

WHAT IS AN ARTIFACT?

Is this stake an artifact?

Explain why or why not.

_____

_____

_____

_____

_____

_____

_____

_____

LOWER PORTAGE CAMP SITE

● Campfire
◉ Campfire
◎ Campfire

▬ Stake
▲ Projectile Point
⬟ Stone Flake
⬮ Bison Bone

N

0,0
SITE
DATUM

Name _____

WHAT CAN YOU TELL ABOUT THE LOWER PORTAGE CAMP SITE?

Fill in the chart below.

Grid Unit	Number of Campfires	Number of Projectile Points	Number of Stone Flakes	Number of Bones

In what grid unit was the stake found? _____

Name _____

SITE STRATIGRAPHY

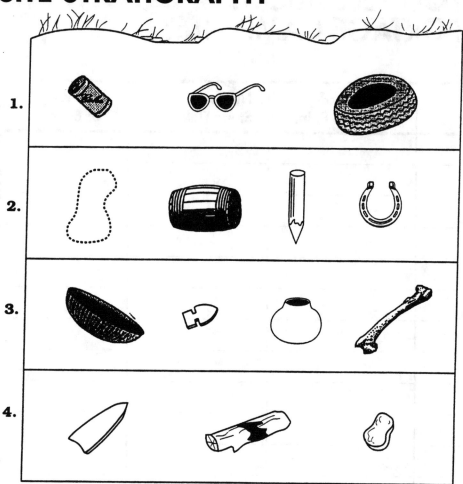

1.   0-30
       years ago

2.   100-200
       years ago

3.   750-1,000
       years ago

4.   10,000-12,000
       years ago

Approximately how old are the artifacts below? Who do you think left each of these artifacts?

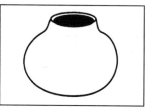

1. _____
   _____

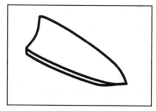

2. _____
   _____

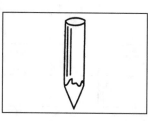

3. _____
   _____

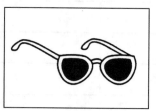

4. _____
   _____

TEACHER'S ANSWER KEY

CHECKING YOUR FACTS
(page 15)
1. Thomas Jefferson
2. France
3. West side of the Rockies
4. $15 million
5. Missouri
6. F
7. F
8. F
9. F
10. T
11. T
12. T
13. T
14. F
15. T

BUYING SUPPLIES
(page 16)
We can make some assumptions about what was important to Lewis and Clark by studying the list of supplies that they brought, the quantities that they chose to take, and what they chose not to take.

Supplies Taken:
50 pounds of pork
Extra food was taken so they could supplement the game they planned to kill along the way.

Fishing line
Fish hooks and line were purchased for the expedition.

5 compasses
Surveying equipment, including compasses, measuring chains, a spirit level, a quadrant, a sextant, and a ship's chronometer (clock), were a priority in order to take the measurements requested by President Jefferson.

2 medicine chests
Two medicine chests, containing more than 20 remedies, were taken by the expedition.

45 hand axes
Axes were taken as tools and given as gifts to the Indians they encountered.

Oilcloth tents
Regulation army tents were taken along—and worn out along the way.

Spare clothing
Clothing was taken, but the expedition members made a great deal of clothing and moccasins out of hides as well.

Trumpets
Tin trumpets were taken to be used to call together the corps.

Gunpowder
A man could survive in the wilderness with a good gun, gunpowder, and lead balls.

Ribbons and beads
Ribbons and beads were among the many gifts Lewis brought to give to the Indians they encountered, and they were also used as trade items.

Blank paper
President Jefferson insisted that the expedition members record all of their discoveries.

30 sheepskins
The sheep skins were purchased and brought along to be later made into portable packs.

Supplies not taken:
15 wooden chairs
Chairs were not included in the list of items they brought with them.

Art supplies
While Lewis brought along ink powder, metal pens, and paper for writing, he did not include any art supplies for painting. Any drawings were done in the journals.

Firewood
Firewood is not listed among their requisitioned supplies. It must have been assumed they would find plenty along the way.

Insect repellent
It is undetermined if insect repellent was listed in their list of requested supplies. Instead, bear grease was used as insect repellent.

200 postage stamps
Stamps were not used on letters in 1804. Letters were sent back from expedition members only when members left the group and returned to Washington, D.C.

5 cameras
Cameras were not taken because they had not yet been invented.

DETAILED DESCRIPTIONS
(page 29)
The following abbreviated journal entries are reprinted from *The Journals of the Lewis and Clark Expedition*, edited by Gary E. Moulton by permission of the University of Nebraska Press.

1. **Lewis's description of a badger:**
July 30, Monday, 1804
Joseph Fields Killed and brought in an Anamale Called by the French Brarow and by the Panies Cho car toochthis Anamale Burrows in the Ground and feeds on Flesh, Bugs, and Vigatables "His Shape and Size is like that of a Beaver, his head mouth &c. is like a Dogs with Short Ears, his Tail and Hair is like that of a Ground Hog, and longer; and lighter. his Internals like the internals of a Hog, his Skin, thick and loose, his Belly is White and the Hair Short, a white Streek from his nose to his Sholders. The toe nails of his fore feet is one Inch &3/4 long, & feet large; the nails of his hind feet 3/4 of an Inch long, the hind feet Small and toes Crooked, his legs are short and when he Moves Just Sufficient to raise his body above the ground.

2. **Lewis's description of a grizzly bear:**
Sunday, May 5th 1805
it was a most tremendous looking animal, and extreemly difficult to kill...We had no means of weighing this monster; Capt. Clark thought he would weigh 500 lbs. for my own part I think the estimate is too

small by 100 lbs.   he measured 8 Feet 7 1/2 Inches from the nose to the extremity of the hind feet , 5 F. 10 1/2 Ins. around the breast 1F 11 I around the middle of the arm, & 3F 11 I around the neck; his tallons which were five in number on each foot were 4 3/8 Inches in length....this bear differs from the common black bear in several respects; it's tallons are much longer and more blont, it's tale shorter, it's hair which is of a redish or bey brown, is longer thicker and finer than that of the black bear.

3. Lewis's description of a big-horned sheep:

May 25th Saturday 1805
as we ascended thr river today I saw several gangs of the big-horned animals...and sent drewyer to kill one..it was somewhat larger that the male of the common deer; the boddy reather thicker deeper and not so long in proportion to it's hight as the common deer; the head and horns of the male are remakably large compared with the other part of the anamal; the whole form is much more delicate that the common goat...the hoof is black & large in proportion, is divided, very open and roundly pointed at the toe like the sheep...the belley, inside of the legs, and extremity of the rump...are white as is also the tail except just as its extremity..which is of a dark brown. The horns are largest at their base, and occupy the crown of the head almost entirely. they are compressed, bent backward and lunated; the surface swelling into wavey rings.

4. Clark's description of a prairie dog:

September 7, 1804
near the foot of this high Nole we discovered a Village of an annamale the french call the Prarie Dog which burrows in the grown...The Village of those little dogs in under the ground a

conisiderable distance ...ther mouth resemble the rabbit, head longer, legs short, & toe nails long ther tail like a(round) Squirrel which they Shake and make chatttering noise ther eyes like a dog, their colour is Gray and skin contains Soft fur.

WHO HAS WHAT? (page 38)

Objects:
1. voyageur's touke
2. bonnet case
3. peace medal
4. fire starter
5. buffalo robe
6. glass beads
7. moccasins
8. folk harp

Objects that corps members brought with them:
Voyager's touke, peace medal, fire starter, glass beads, folk harp

Objects that Lewis and Clark either gave to the Indians as gifts or used as trade goods:
Voyager's hat, peace medal, fire starter, glass beads, folk harp, buffalo robe, moccasins

Objects that the Indians gave in return or traded:
bonnet case, buffalo robe, moccasins

EXPEDITION CHALLENGE (page 52)

1. The United States buys the Louisiana Territory from France.
2. Lewis and Clark establish camp on the Wood River in Illinois.
3. The crew begins traveling up the Missouri River.
4. Lewis and Clark confront the Teton Sioux and continue up the river.
5. Lewis and Clark build Fort Mandan for use as a winter camp.
6. The explorers carry their boats and supplies around the Great Falls of the Missouri.
7. Lewis and Clark arrive at the headwaters of the Missouri.
8. Lewis and Clark obtain horses from the Shoshone and travel overland in search of the Columbia River.
9. The crew goes over the Rocky Mountains at Lolo Pass.
10. The expedition floats down the Columbia River.
11. The expedition reaches the Pacific Ocean.
12. The explorers build Fort Clatsop as a winter camp.
13. Lewis and Clark divide the party: Lewis explores other routes to the Great Falls; Clark explores the Yellowstone River.
14. The crew reunites and arrives in St. Louis.

LOWER PORTAGE CAMP SITE (page 60)

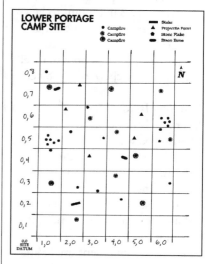

SITE STRATIGRAPHY (page 62)

1. 10,000–12,000
   early humans
2. 750–1,000
   Native Americans
3. 0–30
   recent visitors; campers
4. 100–200
   early settlers